A GUIDE TO
TRADITIONAL
AND MODERN
PAINTING METHODS

A Guide to Traditional and Modern

PAINTING METHODS

Frederic Taubes

A STUDIO BOOK

The Viking Press • New York

First published in 1963 by The Viking Press, Inc.
625 Madison Avenue, New York 22, N.Y.

Published simultaneously in Canada by
The Macmillan Company of Canada Limited

Library of Congress catalog card number: 63-10935
Printed in the U.S.A. by the Murray Printing Co.

Contents

Foreword

The purpose of this book is to discuss the techniques and aesthetics of painting from medieval times to the present, with special emphasis placed on Renaissance, Baroque, and modern styles of painting. Thus the reader may choose the type of painting that interests him most and learn the basic techniques used by the masters.

Today painting takes many forms. There are successful artists who follow or try to follow technically classical traditions; there are those who choose the style of the Impressionists or post-Impressionists; and there are those who more or less ignore past traditions and struggle to achieve some new way of expressing themselves.

There can be no doubt that, whatever type of painting the student endorses and would like to use as the basis for development, he must know basic principles and techniques. Even the abstract artist, to be successful, must be aware of good and bad practices in applying paint to canvas. The student who ignores traditions altogether is merely blinding himself to the opportunities that are offered through a proper understanding of such processes as underpainting or alla prima, of glazing, scumbling, and the use of a painting medium. Such knowledge can facilitate his work and give it permanent value.

It is hoped that readers may find this book useful not only for its technical hints but also as an aid in appreciating various styles of painting and in recognizing inherent characteristics that distinguish one style or period of painting from another.

Craftsmanship is one thing and choice of subject is another. Thus we find painters who employ the techniques of the old masters while painting subjects that were undreamed of in the past. This book does not attempt to influence the reader in any direction; it merely represents an attempt to provide the key with which he may be able to realize his artistic ambitions.

1. Medieval Painting

Although the art of painting was practiced in antiquity, the history of Western art—if we think of a continuity of tradition—dates from the beginning of the thirteenth century. Under the general term "medieval" art, this period may be said to have lasted until the end of the fourteenth century, prior to the beginning of the Italian Renaissance.

Styles. The art of the pre-Renaissance masters is essentially decorative. These painters expressed themselves through the stylization of natural forms; that is to say, they relied upon a convention rather than on the imitation of nature itself. This convention stemmed from the art of Byzantium. Conspicuous characteristics of the style are brightness of color and the absence of realistic perspective, the latter produced an effect of flatness; the Byzantine artist painted figures and other objects on plain backgrounds which might suggest a wall, and he did not introduce any intervening detail or variance of color to give a natural impression of distance. In other words, the backgrounds were merely "filled in" with color, much like the background of a printed fabric or a decoratively painted box.

To set off the figures of their madonnas or saints, Byzantine painters usually used gold leaf, which made their paintings appropriately rich and bright in the dark settings of the churches for which they were designed. It is easy to understand that in the dimly lit interiors of the medieval or pre-medieval church any background other than gold would have been largely lost. The background reflected the candlelight, and the large images enclosed by the gold stood out in a bold, poster-like fashion.

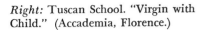

Right: Tuscan School. "Virgin with Child." (Accademia, Florence.)

Left: Cimabue. "Christ the Judge." Mosaic. (Baptistery, Florence.)

The early style of European painting was based on Byzantine conventions. Formalized figures and decorative arrangement of folds, as seen in these two pictures, are characteristic of the style. The folds are not molded but designed. Blending and blurring of colors was not attempted by the Italian primitives; instead, every color area was enclosed by firmly drawn lines which made it distinct from the adjoining areas.

11

While realistic effects may have been intended by these early painters, the limitation of the tempera technique did not permit the naturalism which became both possible and fashionable after the more versatile oil medium came into its own.

It is interesting to note that while the subjects chosen by modern painters are for the most part different from those used by the so-called primitive masters, a stylistic affinity exists in the nonrealistic approach.

Techniques. Pre-Renaissance painting employed a simple, direct technique. Methodical underpaintings were absent, except in cases where the transparent madder lake (an equivalent of our alizarin crimson) or some other transparent color was used. However, the modern painter, in following the primitive or Byzantine style, is not bound by convention and can evolve any technique he desires to achieve the same kind of effect. He may use glazing (the application of a darker transparent color over a lighter underpainting); he can employ scumbling (light, semi-transparent applications used over a dark ground); or he may even use texturing to produce variations in the surface appearance of paint. These variations can be extreme, ranging from thin glazes to excessive thick impasti.

In cases where gold leaf is applied, a rigid support such as a wooden panel or Masonite board should be chosen, as gilding can be done more efficiently on a hard surface. Today, Masonite is usually preferred because a wooden board, being hygroscopic, is apt to warp and check. A thick plywood panel is sometimes used; however, when gessoed, the surface appearance of plywood is no different from that of Masonite. Masonite is more permanent than either a wooden board or a plywood panel. Whatever the surface used, it should always be primed with gesso before painting begins. (General notes on priming are given in Chapter 3.) Gilding should be done over a colored rather than a white surface. A dry pigment, such as ocher or iron oxide red, can be added to color the gesso priming. An extra-smooth gessoed surface is obtained by rubbing it lightly with fine sandpaper.

When a *burnished* gold surface is desired (to achieve a very high gloss), the gesso priming must be prepared from gilders' clay; this white material can also be colored by an ocher or iron oxide red pigment. To bind the clay, a size, made of one ounce of glue or gelatin to one pint of water, is best. This priming should be brushed onto the surface and allowed to dry. Later, when attaching the gold leaf to the clay-gesso surface, simply wet the surface slightly, place the foil on it, and press it down lightly. The high-gloss gilt effect is finally produced by polishing the surface with a burnisher.

In all instances—as when gilding a regular artist's canvas, or any oil-painted surface—*gold size* should be used. This viscous liquid comes ready-made at artists'-material stores and is easily applied with a brush. Allow the surface to dry to a point where it is slightly tacky; then place the foil on it.

Gold leaf should always be cut to the required size with its underlying layer of tissue paper and flipped with this paper onto the surface. Gold leaf is a highly malleable material, and even small bits of it will merge with other small or large bits to make a uniform surface.

Sometimes we may wish to use gold in other than a flat background design. It can be highly effective in small areas or as an outline. This is a very simple process. If you are using the traditional gesso prepared from glue size, pour a little ink into a cup of water and paint the design with a brushed on the gessoed surface; then apply the gold leaf. The ink is added to the water in order to make the brush lines discernible. Another method is to paint the design onto the surface with gold (oil) size; then apply the foil and rub off the loose leaf after the size has dried. This process can be used on any surface. The entire design should be covered with the gold foil, but the foil will adhere only to the water-treated surface. When the surface is dry, rub it with your fingers and the unattached gold will be removed.

Colors. The palette of the pre-Renaissance painters was simple. Besides the earth colors—umber, ocher, sienna, and the iron oxide reds (also lapis lazuli for the blues and verdigris for the greens)—only two manufactured colors were used: white lead and vermilion. The latter color was also obtained in natural state from Spain. Black was obtained from soot.

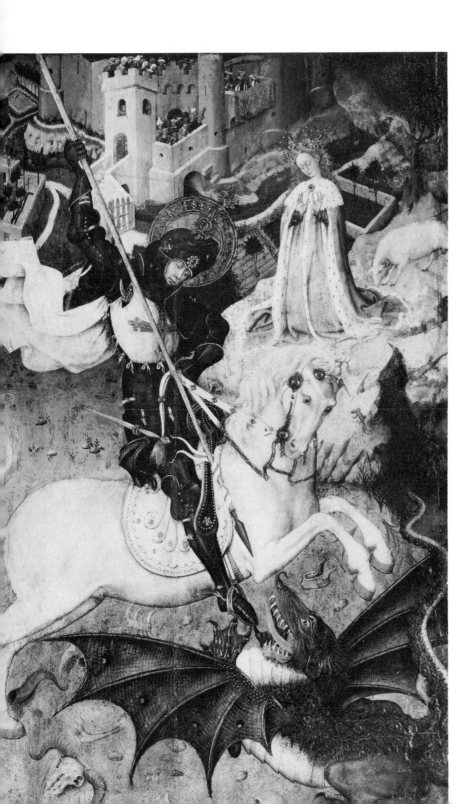

Above: Giovanni di Paolo. "Adoration of the Magi." (National Gallery of Art, Washington.)

Left: Bernardo Martorell. "St. George and the Dragon." (Art Institute of Chicago.)

These compositions show an "illogical" use of perspective. In the fourteenth century the principles of scientific perspective had not yet been established. The rigidity of outline was due largely to use of the tempera medium, which did not allow the free manipulation that became possible later with the introduction of oil paints.

2. Painting from the Renaissance through the Eighteenth Century

The technique of oil painting reached its fullest development at the beginning of the fifteenth century. We may safely say that it was the Flemish painters who actually perfected this technique; however, the methods of many Italians at the middle of the century were technically comparable to those of the Flemish. Toward the end of the century, the methods and materials used by the Italian school underwent various modifications, but these changes did not bring about any technical advance.

Styles. The painting of the Italian Renaissance is less naturalistic than that of the late Gothic (Flemish) school as represented by the van Eyck brothers, Jan and Hubert, and their followers. Italian painting was inspired largely by the classic precepts established during the so-called Golden Age of art in Greece. This poetic concept of beauty involved idealized figures, harmonious proportions, and ease and freedom of execution. Clearly defined details were also part of that style. Instead of the flat backgrounds employed by the Byzantine school, landscapes were frequently included, each area of which was like a separate painting, though skillfully composed to form an integral part of the picture. The Flemish painters worked in much the same way, carrying realistic detail to an even greater point of accuracy than the Italians.

The Renaissance style, beginning with the fifteenth century, ran its course during the following hundred and fifty years. These are, of course, approximate dates, for styles overlapped over long periods of time, depending on the proclivities of artists and the places where they worked.

16

Techniques. The van Eycks are looked upon as the perfectors of the pure oil-painting technique, which relied upon an underpainting, or rather on a succession of underpaintings with opaque and transparent overpaintings. Broadly speaking, the underpainting established the basic composition, and the overpainting or glazes added color while allowing part of the underpainting to show through. The theory that the van Eycks employed a tempera underpainting and oil overpainting or glazing was proved to be erroneous recently through the micro-chemical analysis conducted by Dr. Paul Coremans in Brussels.

A second method of oil painting, called *alla prima,* was brought to fruition by the Flemish painter Hieronymus Bosch, who worked between the years 1475 and 1516. Bosch, although not the first to paint in alla prima, was artistically superior to his predecessors and is therefore probably the best of the earliest artists to study for this technique. It can be looked upon as a one-phase operation, because it aims from the start at the final effect. Painting is done with wet paint on wet paint (usually referred to as wet-on-wet) on a so-called *imprimatura* (a thin, transparent veil of color) and without **any** underpainting. This implies that whatever painting is done has to be finished within a day or two while the surface is still wet; otherwise, if traditional materials are used, the paint will dry in.

Materials. Today many of the ancient pigments are not obtainable on the market. But for every one of the exquisite but now unavailable colors used by the early masters we possess an equivalent, and many of the modern colors are superior to the ancient ones.

The following palette is an approximation of that used by a typical Renaissance master such as Bellini, Titian, or Tintoretto:

"Warm" colors: Naples yellow,* ocher,* raw sienna,* cadmium yellow, cadmium red, Venetian red,* burnt sienna,* burnt (or raw) umber,* ivory black,* alizarin crimson. Flake white.* "Cool" colors: ultramarine, viridian green, Prussian blue.

The paint diluent. The binder for the pigments has always been linseed

---

*Ancient colors. All others are from one hundred to two hundred years old.

The idealized rather than the realistic character of the faces in these pictures is emphasized, and details are subordinated to preserve the feeling of monumentality.

Left: Piero della Francesca. "Angel." (National Gallery, London.)

Right: Botticelli. "Portrait of a Youth." (National Gallery of Art, Washington.)

Jan Gossaert. "Nativity." (National Gallery, London.)

The late Gothic style demonstrated in these two typical Flemish paintings shows a high degree of realism and a minute attention to detail.

oil. However, the "life-blood" of the paints—the diluent, also referred to as the painting medium—has had a varied and often precarious history. An equivalent of the medium used by the old Flemish masters is composed of stand oil (linseed oil thermally processed [polymerized] in the absence of oxygen), raw linseed oil, and a volatile hard-resin varnish prepared from Congo copal. Copal as well as amber (found in many places in central Europe) was well known in the Middle Ages and according to various authorities these resins were used by the painters long before the Renaissance. This is not to say that paint compounded with a proper quantity and quality of linseed oil is deficient and liable to deteriorate more quickly if not "fortified" by a stand-oil-hard-resin compound; but the fact remains that a technique employing paint "just as it comes out of the tube" is limited in the main to opaque painting.

For technical results approaching the work of the old masters a painting medium must be used. The mistake many beginners make is to use turpentine or linseed oil as a thinner for the paints. While this may serve some purposes, the results of its general practice will be a lack of brilliance, texture, and richness. The resinous medium also permits a freer manipulation of the brush and allows glazing. This is discussed at greater length in the next chapter.

3. Tools and Materials

Surfaces. First there is the surface upon which painting is executed. As already mentioned, two categories of support are used, one rigid and the other elastic. The first type we find in a panel, the second in a canvas. The rigid support is more adaptable for the alla prima technique and the second is preferable for work requiring much underpainting. The reason for this preference is that a rather "toothless" surface is suitable for thin painting (the classic alla prima painting is always thin), whereas a "toothy" surface, such as we find on a canvas, works better for underpainting.

Priming. The priming of Masonite panels (the smooth side of the ⅛-inch-thick *untempered* material) is quite simple. The traditional method employs gesso prepared from glue size. The formula for this gesso mixture is one ounce of glue or gelatin mixed with one pint of water and enough whiting and zinc white to make the solution fairly opaque. (A ten-per-cent addition of titanium white will bring about this condition at once.) To serve for oil painting the gesso must be isolated by the size. However, when using Liquitex gesso (a preparation with an acrylic base, made by Permanent Pigments) no sizing is required. Several other ready-mixed sizes are available in the market, but I always use Liquitex gesso, for it is easy to handle and allows the direct application of oil paint to the surface of the panel after it dries. Because of the slick, mechanically even surface of the ready-prepared gesso panels, I do not recommend them.

The traditional procedure of priming a canvas has been with us since the time of the early Renaissance. First the stretched (raw) canvas must be

The surface of a single-primed canvas is usually too coarse to be used without underpainting. In the middle of this sample a second application of white lead was made with a palette knife to fill the interstices of the fabric without depriving it of its tooth.

sized with the gelled material (a good animal glue size in a concentration of seven per cent will gel at normal room temperature) . The size is then spread with a palette knife thinly, thus sealing the interstices of the fabric. If needed, a rough fabric should then be sanded, in which case a repeated sizing will be necessary. Finally, white lead paint (flake white thinned by the Copal Painting Medium to workable consistency) should be worked into the fabric in the thinnest possible application. This procedure can be repeated as required (always on top of a dry surface) to fill the open grain of the fabric.

However, if Liquitex gesso is used, the canvas can be primed without initial sizing, as in the case of the Masonite panel already described.

Ready-prepared canvas sold in art stores carries either one or two primings. This circumstance alone can determine whether one, two, or more underpaintings will be needed. It must be understood that if the texture of the canvas is allowed to remain conspicuous, the final painting will have a "thin" look. For satisfactory results, the interstices on a fabric should be well filled with paint before the actual work of a painting begins.

When the grain (tooth) of the canvas is pronounced, underpainting as well as priming should be done with a painting knife. A brush is not a strong enough tool to force the paint into a rough fabric. There can be no doubt that the old masters used a knife for priming their canvases, although to my knowledge this practice is not mentioned in any of the contemporary accounts.

On a more or less toothless canvas a knife should not be used for underpainting, since the paint moved by the knife would lie on top of the fabric like a sheet and would not provide the requisite anchorage for the strata of overpaints. Consequently, on a smooth surface, only a brush can be used for underpainting. If, in this process, the imprints of the coarse bristle brush appear undesirable, a soft-hair blender (a flat brush made of squirrel hair used for laying in washes in water color) can be used to smooth them out. The marks made by the soft-hair blender are quite shallow, but they will provide sufficient tooth to anchor the subsequent layer of paint. A painting knife can be used, if desired, for final effects, as well as for priming.

Brushes. We must realize that the kind of brushes we now use date only from the beginning of the nineteenth century. Before then, metal ferrules did not exist. Furthermore, the characteristic flat shape of our bristle brush also originated in the nineteenth century. Old masters' bristle brushes were rounder than the equivalent brush of today. However, similar effects can be obtained with modern brushes.

Several types of brushes should be in every artist's equipment. Basic needs include flat bristle brushes (numbers 4-12) and flat sable brushes (the size will depend on the type of work; a miniaturist may need a $\frac{1}{8}$-inch-wide brush, but for general purposes of blending a $\frac{1}{2}$-inch head is sufficient). Also, little known but most useful instruments are the script liners and strip-

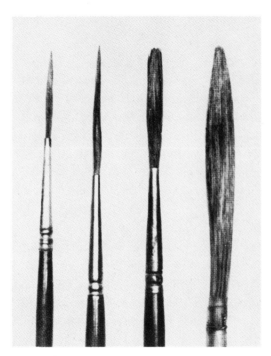

The first two brushes represent script liners; the third is a striper, which, unlike the former, terminates in a flat rather than a pointed tip. The last brush, set in a quill, has an extra-large head.

ers. Unique effects can be produced by these two types of brushes; because of their long body, they can take on large quantities of paint (to work properly, the consistency of paint must be kept flowing). Delineations can be thin or thick depending on the size of the brush and the pressure exerted.

Knives. As already mentioned, painting knives must have been known to the old masters, although for actual painting they do not seem to have been used before the seventeenth century. The spatula type of knife, useful for laying in the gelled size, for priming and underpainting, is, in my opinion, unsuited for anything more than that. The straight-blade knife is the proper tool to use for painting, providing it possesses the right degree of elasticity. Just as we need different kinds of brushes for our work, we should also have more than one kind of palette knife. The three basic types of knives I use are shown here.

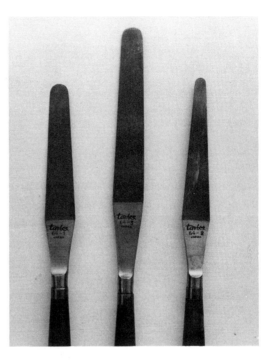

The first knife serves for underpainting, the second for blending colors and for underpainting large surfaces. The third, with its tapering, narrow blade, is most suitable for delicate manipulations of paint.

Paints. Modern paint is deficient in one important respect—the nature of its body. Otherwise, in point of brilliance, color retention, and variety, the best available modern paints would seem to equal and in many cases surpass those used in the past. If the old masters succeeded in achieving better and more lasting color effects than many of the painters of the nineteenth and twentieth centuries this must be ascribed partly to their superior knowledge of the craft and partly to the medium they used as a vehicle for their pigments.

Prior to the machine age, pigments and oil were compounded by hand. However, the painter rarely, if ever, ground the pigments himself: these were prepared by the specialized maker who sold them to the painters in powder form, ready to be turned into paint. (It should be noted that "pigment" always refers to *dry* color, as opposed to "paint," which is pigment mixed with a binder and ready for use.)

27

In early days, paints were not packaged in air-tight receptacles such as the tubes we buy today. The action of air on the drying oil (linseed oil) causes oxidation, and this is responsible for a condition in the oil known as polymerization, which makes the body of paint *viscous.*

Modern tube paint lacks viscosity, not only because the oil used for binding the pigments is neutral (of low acid value) and unpolymerized but because it contains an additive (aluminum stereate) that effectively counteracts the viscous condition. At the same time it allows the pigment to remain in permanent suspension with the oil. Without this stabilizer (or other suitable ingredients), the oil and the pigment would separate, making it impossible to store paint in tubes for indefinite lengths of time. Hence, tube paint is nonviscous, or as we call it, "short." By adding polymerized oil to the paint we can make it viscous, or "long."

Oil Painting Mediums. Taking a cue from the medieval monk Theophilus, who was the first to leave a precise account of the preparation of oils and paints, I have managed to re-establish formulas that were current even before the times of the van Eycks, and that were responsible for the creation of classic paintings of unsurpassed permanence and beauty.

These formulas have now been available for a long time under the name of "Copal Painting Medium" (light and heavy—the first is less viscous than the second), "Copal Concentrate," and "Copal Varnish." They are manufactured by Permanent Pigments, and are generally available in artists'-material stores. However, several different brands of Copal painting mediums are available, but some, because of different composition, may act differently. The media serve, as the term implies, for thinning of the tube paint while painting. Oil paint, being of dense consistency, often requires considerable dilution by the medium. Sometimes, as in glazing, this consistency may approximate that of water color. The concentrate should be added to each of the colors after they have been squeezed from the tubes onto the palette. This oil-and-resin compound changes the brilliance and accelerates the drying of the paint. The medium should not be used for underpainting, because in the lower layers of a painting it serves no useful purpose. However,

(A) Short (non-viscous) paint when heaped up forms sharp and crisp surface contours. Brush strokes made with such paint have a hard, brittle appearance.

(B) Long paint (paint with a high capacity to flow) is smooth-edged, stringy, and supple; it has always the tendency to seek its level. These conditions become more pronounced with the increased content of polymerized oil.

Rembrandt. "Old Woman Cutting Her Nails." Detail. (Metropolitan Museum of Art, New York.)

This detail of Rembrandt's painting shows soft, round edges, which indicate unmistakably the use of a polymerized oil. Whether a hard resin went into the compound of the painting medium, has not, to my knowledge, been verified.

30

its use does not prohibit additional overpainting when this is required.

Before the procedures are discussed in detail, it should be stated that linseed oil, the best binder for pigments, is in many respects inadequate as a paint thinner (or medium) because of three principal considerations. First of all, it has low degree of viscosity; second, it fails to attach itself properly to the canvas when mixed with paint to a liquid consistency; and third, it has a tendency to yellow regardless of its quality and the degree of its purification. This tendency becomes more noticeable with extensive use, such as in glazing.

As a binder for pigments linseed oil, as stated before, is perfectly adequate; however, a minimum quantity is used in the average tube paint, because the manufacturer tries to give the painter the maximum amount of pigment. In other words, he cuts down on the oil content. However, there is nothing easier than to mix a painting medium with the tube colors and thus improve the bond of the pigments.

Painters often use turpentine as a thinner, but this is inappropriate. Turpentine destroys the cohesion of the paint film and makes it brittle, and also prevents it from receiving a proper coat of varnish.

Another common fault is to mix soft resin such as damar or mastic varnish with the oil paint. The surface of such a painting remains susceptible to damage if treated even with the mildest solvent when the time comes for it to be cleaned. Instead, copal resin should be used to give the painting permanence and resistance to cleaning agents.

The Characteristics of Copal Concentrate. This material, used to make the paint more viscous, is a thick honey-like substance combining copal resin and stand oil. A little of it (the size of a small bean) should be scooped up from the bottle with the palette knife and well mixed with about one inch of *each color as it comes from the tube*—advice given already by Theophilus. Only flake white should receive a considerably larger amount of the substance to make it flow. Whereas all the other colors become more liquid when mixed with the concentrate, white lead, because of a chemical reaction, stiffens when a small amount of concentrate is added.

The more concentrate that is added to the paint, the more the colors will assume the character of enamel; hence the amount used should be regulated according to the painter's requirements. The addition of concentrate makes every color appear more brilliant. After mixing the above, paints are then thinned with the painting medium as desired.

Viscosity of Paints. Viscosity refers to the capacity of a liquid to flow; the less viscous the paint, the more free its flow. This in itself is not the only important quality in a painting medium. Stand oil (depending on the degree of its polymerization) can be extremely viscous, and, in spite of its superior qualities such as non-yellowing and the toughness of its linoxyn, it offers too many limitations to be perfectly satisfactory. Thus in choosing the medium we must consider the viscosity plus the capacity to attach itself to the support (when used thinly), as well as other working qualities.

The condition of "attachability" which arises due to the presence of the resin in the medium has already been mentioned. As to the desirability of viscosity, this condition promotes fusion and blending of colors in a manner hardly attainable when working with a diluent such as the raw linseed oil. Moreover, it allows the painter to work wet-on-wet with ease, superimpose wet applications one on top of the other without churning up the underlying paint strata, and altogether to create effects that are comparable to those of the Flemish masters.

4. Traditional Methods of Underpainting

In discussing traditional methods, I do not mean to imply that we, today, could follow the classic precepts exactly. For one thing, identical materials are not readily available. However, we can make very close approximations of early styles and techniques. Modern materials, on the whole, are more reliable, and in using them we may consider any technique that seems necessary to achieve the effects obtained by the old masters.

When painting on canvas the old masters used underpainting, and more often than not they used several underpaintings. The purpose of underpainting is: (1) to build up textures, or simply to create a solid body of paint, a quality which has its own intrinsic beauty; (2) to enhance color through utilization of glazes; and (3) to clarify the artist's ideas while laying the framework for the final painting. Sometimes one and sometimes two or more underpaintings are used to achieve this. Once the groundwork is laid, the final effects can be painted more rapidly and spontaneously, or meticulous details can be executed with much greater ease.

It should be remembered that all overpainting must be done on a *dry* underpainting. A thin underpainting will dry, under normal conditions, in two or three days (more quickly when umber is used), but a heavy layer of paint will require a longer period. Such a layer can be tested for dryness by probing its surface with a fingernail. If the surface paint is hard, another layer of paint can be added.

There is no need to mix a medium (such as copal) with paint for an underpainting; however, a proper medium is imperative when commencing the final painting. By "final" is meant the *intended* final appearance, for

Below: "Portrait Study" in grisaille, by the author.

This illustration shows a portrait executed in grays before it was overpainted in full colors. Depending on the particular habit of the painter, one or more successive grisailles can be applied (always when the preceding painting has dried), until the likeness has been sufficiently developed. Then the final painting is made in full colors. This should also be done on a perfectly dry surface.

Left: Hans Memling. "Madonna." Detail.

This Flemish painting was done in the second half of the fifteenth century. The underpainting is in *grisaille.* As described in the text, the neutral tone of grisaille can be cool or warm gray, pink, or pale green. The flesh in this picture would have been modeled in monotones first, and the true colors superimposed on top of the underpainting after it had dried. In the underpainting not the final colors but their weaker equivalents were used by the old masters on all objects. For example: under red, pink would have been placed; under strong green, a pale green; and so on. A modern modification of this method enlarges upon the traditional technique by calling for underpainting in contrasting color—pink under blue, green under red, etc. First, a precise drawing was made on the gesso of the panel, and every object in the painting was carefully and smoothly underpainted in successive stages. Perhaps three or four underpaintings were used successively to develop all the details shown.

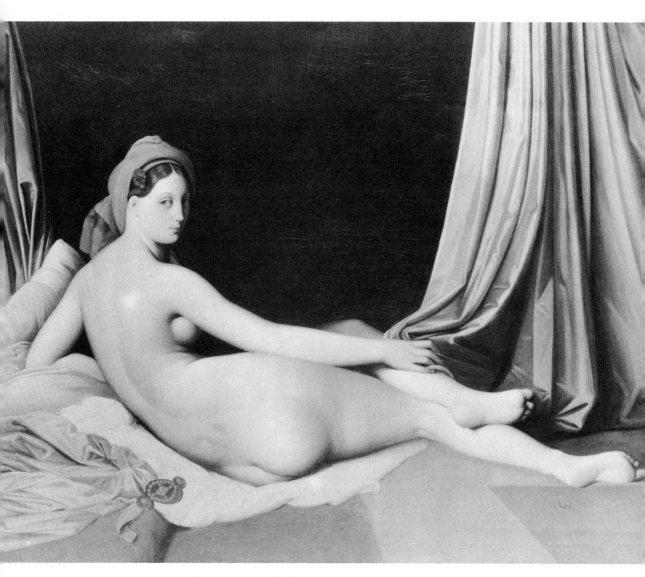

Ingres. "Odalisque en Grisaille." (Metropolitan Museum of Art.)

A nineteenth-century painting carried out entirely in cool grays. Evidently Ingres planned to use transparent colors in the draperies. As there is little shadow on the body, the gray modeling would have been overpainted in predominantly opaque colors. Flesh as seen in light cannot show underlying transparencies simply because it requires the use of white paint, which is opaque. *Thus only the shadows are treated in a transparent manner.* Here only a little white is mixed with the dark colors.

there can of course follow many changes or corrections. The oil medium increases the fluency of the brush strokes and promotes the fusion of colors. Moreover, it allows the painting to dry with the requisite gloss.

Underpainting for Transparent Colors.

Glazes. For glazing, the underpainting must be kept light, because the glaze (applied on top of it) is made up of a darker transparent color. In practice almost every color but the lightest can be used for a glaze provided it has been sufficiently diluted by an oil medium. *"True" glazes are never mixed with white because white reduces transparency.* The only exception to this rule is when painting flesh. Here a certain amount of white must be used for painting shadows—even transparent ones—because when the colors are used thinly even a semi-opaque application will retain some transparency, and this is all that is required of a glaze used for painting flesh.

Glazes must be planned; they cannot be improvised, because the color of the underpainting conditions the color of the glaze. The two must work together to produce an intended effect. For example, black glaze on top of a yellow surface will appear green; a viridian green glaze over red will look grayish; and so on. Glazing always requires that the underpainting be allowed to dry first.

Scumbling. When we reverse the above process and paint a lighter color over a darker one in a semi-transparent manner, the effect is called a "scumble." The effects of scumbling are seldom seen in the earliest Renaissance paintings, but are found frequently in the works of Tintoretto and Goya and other painters from the seventeenth century on. In modern painting the use of scumbling is far more common than the use of glazes, simply because scumbling lends itself to free improvisation. While glazing calls for a light (and dry) underpainting, scumbling is best done into a *wet* surface, and a dark wet color can be applied to an underpainting at any time, regardless of its color.

Characteristic Underpainting Processes. Renaissance painters
such as Botticelli, Bellini, and Raphael employed light underpaintings and

Tintoretto. "Christ on the Sea of Galilee." (National Gallery of Art, Washington.)

This magnificent picture shows strong evidence of a red underpainting. Colors were scumbled thinly on top of the underpainting.

El Greco. "Gethsemane." (National Gallery, London.)

Although a product of the same school as Tintoretto, El Greco employed a slightly different method. In most instances his paintings were done on a smaller scale. The painting ground was the same as Tintoretto's—a dark red—but his underpaintings were more elaborate. According to an account by the contemporary painter and writer Francisco Pacheco (Velázquez' father-in-law), a careful underpainting preceded the final painting. Thus in its initial stages a picture like this was much more "tame" than it appears in its finished form. To quote Pacheco directly: "Who would believe, for instance, that El Greco took his paintings in hand many times, retouching them over and over again, in order to give them those cruel alla prima strokes, feigning valor?"

kept them more or less in warm monotones. These painters used glazes liberally and scumbles very rarely. All underpaintings were done in oil colors.

Later Renaissance (or early Baroque) painters such as Titian, Tintoretto, and other Venetian masters worked, predominantly, on canvases primed with dark colors such as umber, gray, and dark red. Sometimes painting was done in alla prima fashion, and sometimes traditional underpaintings were used. Alla prima painting on a transparent imprimatura (veil of color) was a Flemish invention, perfected by Hieronymus Bosch and later employed by Brueghel and Rubens.

The late Baroque painters, such as Tiepolo and Guardi, underpainted in light colors such as pink, pale gray, blue, and green. These colors were strongly intermixed with white; hence we can refer to them as pastel hues. Goya, who straddles the eighteenth and nineteenth centuries, combined all the techniques of the preceding ages, with the chief accent on scumbling rather than on glazing.

The seventeenth, eighteenth, and nineteenth centuries (before the advent of the Impressionists), produced no significant innovations or improvements upon the older methods of oil painting.

Opposite: Hieronymus Bosch. "The Last Judgment." Detail. (Alte Pinakothek, Munich.)

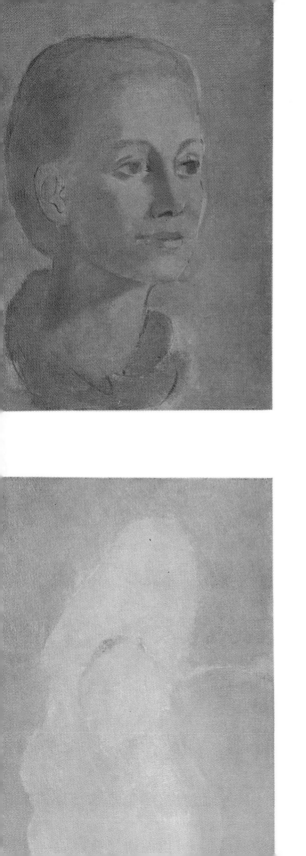

5. Classic Painting: Step by Step

In this chapter the two basic categories of painting are demonstrated step by step. In the first category, underpainting processes (illustrated by a portrait and a landscape) are presented in as close an approximation to the early masters as possible; in the second, painting without an underpainting (the alla prima technique) is demonstrated in the two typical variations.

Underpainting.

Portrait Study. The head on the opposite page was first outlined with charcoal over an even gray ground produced from umber, white, and Prussian blue. The drawing was made permanent by spraying it with fixative. The outline of the head could have been done just as well with a sable brush using an oil color such as umber or burnt sienna thinned with turpentine. The painting was then carried out in grisaille on top of the drawing. The gray differed in hue from the painting ground so the tones would register clearly. However, the hair was underpainted with ocher and white, with some umber added in the shadow area. Upon drying, this underpainting was oiled with painting medium. Directly after this, and while the surface was still wet, the overpainting was started.

The following colors were used for the shadow areas: umber, Venetian red, ocher, ultramarine blue, and white. The colors were mixed together and

Opposite: Two stages in a portrait and a landscape painting by the author. See text above and on page 44.

applied thinly so that the gray underpainting showed through. For the light areas white and ocher were mostly used, and some umber was added to tone down the light colors where needed. The hair was glazed with umber mixed with ultramarine blue (without white). In the lightest areas of the hair the paint was simply wiped off with a cheesecloth allowing the original color (ocher) of the underpainting to serve for the highlights. For the background area umber, ultramarine, ocher, and white were used. Besides white, the range of colors for the entire painting consisted of umber, Venetian red, ocher, and ultramarine. With two or three additional colors an elaborate color scheme for the dress and background could have been worked out. The overpainting (on top of the grisaille) was finished in one operation while painting wet on wet.

There are no rules against the use of a second or third overpainting which might be required to correct a likeness, or to add more details should they later seem desirable. If the areas in shade become opaque (as they will when repeatedly overpainted), a scumble will invariably relieve the opacity. (See Chapter 4.)

Landscape Study. The composition at the bottom of page 42 was sketched with a script liner brush on a white primed canvas, using burnt sienna thinned with turpentine. (Where multicolored effects are desired, the use of a toned gray ground is inappropriate. White heightens the key of the superimposed colors, whereas a dark ground tends to lower it.) Next, the sky was underpainted in pink, made from a mixture of Venetian red and white. For the distance and middle ground, a light range of green-gray color was used, the lightest shade being reserved for the distance and a slightly darker one for the middle ground. These colors were mixed from umber, Prussian blue, ocher, and viridian green. The rock in the foreground was underpainted in a mixture of ocher, umber, and white.

When this first underpainting had dried properly (it took three days) the drawing, which had become largely obliterated, was developed in greater detail using burnt sienna diluted with turpentine. There followed another underpainting in which the vaguely sketched masses (lacking definite shape and color) were more clearly defined. This second underpainting did not differ much from the first one in point of color, except for a clearer definition of the composition and a richer texture resulting from the superimposed heavier paint layer.

The final painting, in which nearly all the details were added, was done quite rapidly, using a palette knife, script liners, and round sable brushes. · Bristle brushes were used merely for the initial laying in of colors. The range of colors used for the final overpainting were: Naples yellow, ocher, cadmium yellow, Venetian red, burnt sienna, burnt umber, ultramarine, viridian green, and white.

General Notes on Classic Underpainting. For a portrait, the ground should be painted in one of the following four colors: a light, cool, gray (Prussian blue, umber, and white); a warm gray (umber and white); a gray-green (Prussian blue, umber, ocher, and white); or pink (Venetian red and white). The underpainting of flesh should be in neutral color—grisaille, also known as dead-coloring. In considering the color of clothes, draperies, and other accessories their weaker equivalents should be used, or for a stronger effect contrasting colors should be employed, such as red under black or green, green under red, etc.

In the case of landscape and still-life work, the underpainting should be done on a white primed surface, predominantly in light colors chosen according to the particular requirements of the subject matter and general effect desired. In practice the planned colors can usually only be guessed at, because one can seldom completely previsualize the final appearance of a painting. In the days of the Renaissance, paintings were well planned in advance and the artist carried out all the steps methodically. Today, however, we rely to a much greater extent on improvisation.

As a general rule, contrasting colors are a good choice for underpainting. For skies (under blue), pink, gray, or a yellowish color can be used to good effect; for trees, grass, and the like (under green) yellow is usually the best choice. For red motifs an underpainting of green, yellow, or orange is suitable, depending upon the shade of red and the brightness required. A predomi-

Hieronymus Bosch. "Temptation of St. Anthony." Detail. (Royal Museum, Brussels.)

nantly gray-green color is always a good choice when used under areas representing water or rock. In cases where the final effect cannot be pre-visualized, neutral colors in various shades of gray, yellow, green, or pink are the safest choice for the underpainting.

Alla Prima Painting. Late in the fifteenth century the alla prima technique was perfected by Bosch, as already stated, and it was later used almost exclusively by Brueghel. It was also preferred by Rubens in most of the paintings done by his own hand.

The Dutch painter and author Karel van Mander explained Bosch's

46

These details from paintings by Bosch were done on wooden panels covered with gesso. The first carries an ocher imprimatura, and the second burnt sienna and ocher. Both were painted alla prima.

Hieronymus Bosch. "The Mocking of Christ." Detail. (Royal Museum, Brussels.)

Pieter Brueghel. "The Tower of Babel." (Kunsthistorisches Museum, Vienna.)

This painting demonstrates essentially the same method used by Bosch, but Brueghel varied the color of the imprimatura, according to the final color of the subject. A grayish color is in evidence under portions of the rocks, and ocher was used to enhance the final effect of water.

49

Above: Peter Paul Rubens. "Marcus Aurelius." Detail. (Metropolitan Museum of Art.)

Left: Peter Paul Rubens. "The Triumph of Christ over Sin and Death." (Metropolitan Museum of Art, New York.)

On small panels such as these two, Rubens' alla prima technique appears at its best. The original color of the imprimatura (ocher) is in evidence throughout both paintings. In the areas of the architectural frame of the first example, the details have been carried out in a draftsmanlike fashion, and the color of the imprimatura was used for the light parts. The darks consist of umber glazes. The character of this area as well as of the background suggest water color rather than oil painting, inasmuch as glazes predominate. The only opaque color is the white used in the second example, which makes the sketchiness of the treatment still more pronounced.

51

technique this way: "He made his drawings of subjects on the white ground of his panels, over which he painted a transparent layer in a color, or in a shade more or less like flesh. Frequently he used the ground for part of the final effect of the painting." In other words, the painting did not completely cover the transparent initial color spread over the white gesso. This initial color is called imprimatura.

Technique. Gesso is the best priming for painting alla prima and a Masonite panel the most durable and practical support. The gesso applied to the smooth side of the Masonite will, in spite of its relative smoothness, possess a slight "tooth" formed by the pigment from which it is made. However, this "tooth" will not impede the movements of the brush, as would be the case on a "normal" medium-rough canvas. But if the canvas is smooth, that is, practically "toothless" (and as such it would not be well adaptable for underpainting), it can also be used for alla prima technique.

The step-by-step procedure in alla prima work is as follows: (1) A drawing is made on the white gesso, or on the imprimatura (see below). This sketch can be done with charcoal, crayon, or pencil and made indelible by means of a fixative; or it can be done in ink. (2) The imprimatura (with the drawing) should be covered thinly by the Copal Painting Medium, and all painting should be done in one operation on this wet surface. One should always endeavor to maintain transparencies, allowing the imprimatura to assert itself here and there; or, as van Mander would have said, the ground should often show through as part of the final effect. However, one should always paint on *dry* imprimatura. When copal varnish is used, the imprimatura will become sufficiently resistant to the action of a turpentine-containing medium in two days.

All the colors used for alla prima technique should be conditioned with a medium such as Copal Concentrate (discussed in Chapter 3) or, with a highly polymerized stand oil to give the paint greater viscosity and a heavier body.

Variations. Alla prima is the fastest way of painting, and since some

Peter Paul Rubens. "Venus before a Mirror." (Duke of Liechtenstein Collection.)

Although much of this painting is alla prima work, glazes appear in the shadows, the hair, and small parts of the background. Thus the total effect of the painting is predominantly opaque and does not have the characteristics of alla prima work.

painters, such as Tintoretto, had to cover enormous surfaces speedily, they too employed alla prima techniques, but these were of a different kind. In the case of Tintoretto and other masters including El Greco, Frans Hals, and Rembrandt, it was executed on a dark, opaque ground. On such ground glazing was, of course, impossible, but the dark surfaces were especially adapted for scumbling and for opaque painting, which characterizes the work of the Venetian Baroque masters.

For an imprimatura, any desirable color can be used. However, the more transparent colors such as burnt sienna, umber, viridian, ocher, and cadmium yellow are the most frequently used. These colors should be thinned with varnish to water-color consistency. A brand of varnish especially formulated for this operation is Copal Varnish. Other brands may require thinning with turpentine to be workable for making an imprimatura. (A color thinned with a soft resin varnish, such as damar or mastic, will dissolve regardless of how long it has been allowed to dry.)

Summary. As a support, a panel is the preferable choice, and this should be primed with gesso and allowed to dry. The initial coloring (imprimatura) is next applied. This should be sufficiently thin so that the white of the gesso shows through, making the colors appear luminous. The imprimatura can be prepared from any desired color except white and Naples yellow —the lightest colors on our palette. Several colors can be used simultaneously (each applied with a clean brush), depending on the intention of the painter and the subject matter at hand. The painting should be accomplished while painting wet-on-wet in one operation, and enough of the original imprimatura should remain in evidence so that the painting remains well integrated and harmonious in its total effect.

Opposite: Tintoretto. "Crucifixion." Detail. (Scuola di San Rocco, Venice.)

Tintoretto always painted on canvas, using a dark red priming which was usually made up of Venetian red and umber. I don't know whether a chemical analysis of such priming has been made, but my belief is that Tintoretto used flake white with the red in order to provide the ground with requisite leanness. This technique permits great spontaneity because brush strokes of a light color show clearly on a dark surface. Tintoretto worked approximately as follows: he left the original ground largely untouched for the darkest effects, and used a lighter, more or less opaque scumble for the middle tones. Once the highlights were established, the plasticity of the painting became dramatically apparent. This manner of painting is not unlike pastel painting done on dark paper. When he worked on a small scale, his method was more complex.

Above: Goya. "The Infanta Maria Luisa." (Metropolitan Museum of Art.)

The priming used for this painting is lighter than that used by Tintoretto. Its orange color can be considered as a middle tone. As in the Frans Hals "Portrait of a Painter," it mediates between light and shade. For example, the shadow of the face of the child represents the original orange color of the priming. The deepest shadows on the figure of Maria Luisa are mere glazes, and the light is painted with white mixed with a little ocher. An approximation of the flesh color used by Goya would call for umber, ultramarine, or black, with Venetian red (or cadmium red), ocher, and white for the shadow areas. For the light areas white, ocher, and cadmium red could be used.

Left: Frans Hals. "Portrait of a Painter." (Frick Collection, New York.)

The bravura evident in the work of this Dutch master is unparalleled. He was capable of painting a portrait in alla prima, but sometimes his clients' demands for a meticulous finish forced him to become more elaborate. In consequence, such works lack Hals' usual vigor and spontaneity. This portrait in my opinion was created in a day—perhaps in less than eight hours. The nature of the toned canvas (Hals used a cool brown, somewhat lighter than the shadows of the flesh) greatly facilitated the progress of work.

Joachim Patinir. "Saint Jerome." (National Gallery, London).

One of the great landscape painters, Patinir, tells a story using landscape motifs alone. Here our eyes are led as in a book of fables over a panorama of magnificent scenes. Typical of fifteenth-century landscapes is the high horizon line, which makes it seem as if the scene is viewed from above.

6. Composition in Classic Painting

Any grouping of objects with a three-dimensional effect can be looked upon as a "composition." When referring to composition as opposed to design—in the conventional use of the term—every composition (arrangement of motifs) takes into account space in depth.

Medieval Painting. Deep space was not stressed in medieval painting. Instead of showing recession in depth, primitive painters used a vertical progression—that is to say, they placed their motifs one above another. This tendency influenced the fourteenth-century artists, whose landscapes are distinguished by a horizon placed high on the painting's plane. Hence, in paintings such as those by the van Eycks and their followers, landscapes appear to us as if seen from above. This allowed the arists to include many storytelling details in the background. The relation between the areas of sky and ground is of great importance in the composition of a landscape, for it is one of the determinants of its style. The early narrative style incorporating an abundance of detail demanded a linear approach with the horizon high on the picture plane. From the sixteenth century on, artists dropped the horizon to an increasingly lower plane.

Renaissance Painting. In principle, the compositions of the Renaissance are built along vertical and horizontal lines. The construction of motifs is, predominantly, frontal, and in spite of occasional animation the effect tends to appear static.

The greatest innovation of the Renaissance school (Italian as well as

Meindert Hobbema. "The Avenue, Middelharnis." (National Gallery, London.)

In contrast to the preceding example this Dutch landscape, painted in the seventeenth century, has the horizon placed low on the picture plane, thus allowing the sky to dominate the scene. Hence we have here a worm's-eye view rather than the bird's-eye view which was characteristic of earlier masters.

Titian. "Venus and the Lute Player." (Metropolitan Museum of Art.)

The painter who follows classic tenets observes the principles of empirical perspective; he is concerned with clarity in the definition of form, and stresses the monumentality and dignity of the human figure. This kind of realism might be termed "ideal," for it avoids distorted and violent color and chiaroscuro effects. In his later paintings, Titian usually worked over a dark red ground. He used light underpaintings chiefly in areas of the flesh, and in draperies which were to receive glazes.

62

El Greco. "Baptism of Christ."
(Prado Museum, Madrid.)

El Greco is considered to be a Man-
nerist, although today we often refer
to him as an Expressionist. All the
characteristics of mannerism prevail
in this painting: strong, illogical
clashes of light and dark, distortions
of anatomy, and an acid and eccentric color. The linear definitions
are for emphasis rather than outline.

Giovanni Bellini. "Allegory." (Uffizi Gallery, Florence.)

Space appears arranged according to empirical perspective; that is, the scene is viewed from a single focus. In this kind of perspective all parallels meet on the horizon, which lies at eye level. The harmonious relationships shown here fully illustrate Leon Battista Alberti's precepts of Renaissance composition: "The task of congruity is to put together members differing from one another in their nature in such a manner that they may conspire to form a beautiful whole."

Tintoretto. "Annunciation." (Scuola di San Rocco, Venice.)

Here, as in so many paintings of the late sixteenth century, light and shade are used not for clarification of forms, but rather for achieving a dramatic effect.

Flemish) was the discovery of a measurable space—predicated on the so-called scientific, empirical, or realistic perspective. The principle of this kind of perspective is to view the scene from one vantage point along lines that meet on the horizon at eye level. In this system linear perspective is linked with aerial perspective, the one qualifying the other to the extent that a certain color (progressing along the lines that recede into the background) will change its hue according to its proximity or distance from the foreground. The change in all colors due to atmospheric conditioning expresses itself in a weakening of the key of each color, and its eventual fade-out to a uniform, pale bluish or greenish hue. A system which acknowledges this change is labeled "atmospheric perspective." With minor variations and modifications, this system of aerial perspective, as seen in the landscapes of Patinir and other masters, prevailed until the advent of post-Impressionism.

Baroque Painting. The system of composition adopted in the late sixteenth century differed radically in many respects from that of the early or high Renaissance. Linear perspective gave way to an ambiguous conception of space. However, the principle of the color fade-out remained the same. The general state of repose in the earlier paintings changed to one of turbulence. When a painting by Piero della Francesca is compared to one by Rubens, this dramatic change of style is at once recognized. Firm outlines of figures became fuzzy, every detail appeared to be in motion, the axial system of horizontals and verticals upon which earlier compositions were built changed into the serpentine, and the symmetric and solid forms became asymmetric and fluid. This is well demonstrated in the work of such painters as El Greco and Tintoretto.

Other characteristics of the Baroque style as well as the period immediately preceding it, known as Mannerism, are a tendency toward exaggeration and over-dramatization in regard to proportions, the movement of figures, the use of light and shade, and a change in the use of color.

7. Light and Shade in Classic Painting

In using the term "classic painting," I continue to refer to the paintings of the Renaissance period. However, the same principles and techniques were employed up to the nineteenth century, before the advent of Impressionism.

One of the most important principles in classic painting is the rendering of light and shade. This is referred to as *chiaroscuro*. The first conscious differentiation between light and shade appeared during the high Renaissance, but it was not until the Baroque period that the dramatic potentialities of these relationships were fully developed. Through the emphasis of light and shade the plastic appearance of objects was heightened and their three-dimensional quality was stressed. By submerging parts of the motifs in shade, by obscuring objects or parts of objects, classic artists created both realistic and highly dramatic effects. A typical example is shown in the Rembrandt painting illustrated on page 72.

The proportion of light and shade in different paintings varies. Either the light area or the area of shadows can predominate, or the areas of light and shade can be balanced. Moreover, the light can enter the scene at a different angle—from the top or from the sides. The higher the source of light (I refer here to outdoor light, not a studio skylight), the more sober, as a rule, the mood of the scene. With the declining sun, the light can glorify even the most trivial subject. This is well demonstrated in the work of Guardi and Belotto.

Opposite: Mathias Grünewald. "Resurrection." (Isenheim Altar, Colmar, France.)

Exaggerated contrasts of searing lights and deep shadows are used again in this painting to produce a dramatic effect. Here we may even speak of a modern use of chiaroscuro as adopted by some of the Expressionists.

Jan Vermeer. "The Painter at Work in His Studio." (Count Czernin Collection, Vienna.)

Light illuminates only small segments of this scene. Intermediate areas, the so-called middle tones, are not stressed. Light meets dark in sharp contrasts.

Leonardo da Vinci. "Madonna of the Rocks." Detail. (National Gallery, London.)

An over-all, mellow, balanced relationship of light and shade is typical of high Renaissance painting. This clarifies rather than obscures forms. In Leonardo's work, all the subtleties inherent in chiaroscuro are demonstrated for the first time. None of his followers achieved comparable delicacy in the treatment of light and shade. Leonardo described this effect as *sfumato*—like a coil of smoke that starts with considerable density and becomes imperceptibly thinner and thinner until it vanishes into the atmosphere.

Opposite: Rembrandt. "The Concord of the States." Detail. (Boyman's Museum, Rotterdam.)

The shadow areas in this painting far exceed the areas of light, hence the mood of "mystery." Out of the all-enveloping darkness the light creates eerie contrasts.

Right: Corot. "Hagar in the Wilderness." (Metropolitan Museum.)

The technique used here is strictly academic, lacking refinement and differentiation in point of texture, opacity, and transparency. It possesses neither the virtue of simplicity, such as seen in his early Italian landscapes, nor the characteristic feathery appearance that distinguishes Corot's later work.

Painting Areas Obscured by Shadows. More often than not, classic precepts of painting technique call for transparent shadows in keeping with their veil-like appearance. Should one wish to paint the shadows in a transparent manner, *the underpainting must be kept light.* The lighter the underpainting is, the more luminous the shadows will appear.

In preparing the underpainting for the areas in shadow, two considerations should be kept in mind—its solidity and its color. As to the solidity, it must be remembered that glazes, traditionally, have no body of their own; they are made up largely of the medium with very little paint added. Therefore, as a preliminary for the glaze, it is important to build up several layers of underpaintings so that the interstices of the fabric are filled in completely. On a commercially prepared canvas, glazes revealing the mechanically even grain of the weave are especially unattractive. The color of the underpainting is equally important. It should be remembered that the higher or lighter its key and the more yellow its hue, the more luminous the dark glaze will appear on top of it. If a gray underpainting is used, the strength of the glaze will be weaker. The darker and grayer the underpainting, the dimmer the effect of the final painting.

Belotto. "Freyung Square, Vienna." (Kunsthistorisches Museum, Vienna.)

The realistic representation of this city vista is highly romanticized, according to common custom in mid-eighteenth-century painting. Long shadows are cast by objects illuminated by the declining sun.

Opposite: Rembrandt. "Self-Portrait." Detail. Rembrandt was a master of glazes and impasti. Here the brush marks crisscross in several heavy overpaints, contrasting with thinly applied glazes.

8. The Treatment of Contours

All painting before the high Renaissance (i.e., Byzantine, medieval, and paintings of the fifteenth century) relied on linear contour. The broken or fuzzy contour, often refererred to as "painterly," was first practiced in the sixteenth century by Titian. Linear contour indicates that forms are confined within a rigid outline. Early artists used this technique, and by drawing tight lines around each form tended to isolate it from its surroundings. To use a "painterly" approach means to soften the contours to a greater or lesser extent, allowing the objects to merge to an extent with the background.

Contours can be handled very differently. An object can have a thin, wirelike outline, as in Byzantine painting, or it can meet its surrounding area at a hard, unyielding border without an actual outline, as in a painting by Botticelli.

The object can lose its contour and merge in certain areas with its surroundings, as in the work of Rembrandt. Finally, a contour may serve the purpose of emphasis, as especially favored by modern artists. The differences between these conceptions are demonstrated in the following illustrations.

Opposite: El Greco. "Adoration of the Shepherds." Detail. (Metropolitan Museum of Art.)

Lucas Cranach. "Judgment of Paris." (State Museum, Copenhagen.)

Stylistically, these two paintings stand at opposite poles. In Cranach's conception, every detail, because of isolation by outlines, is independent of its surrounding. In fact, what we see in his composition is pictures within pictures—motifs that have self-contained, independent life. The unvaried, hard contours are in perfect harmony with the archaic style of the composition. In El Greco's painting the contours are treated to make one object enter into relationship with its surroundings. Their character is predicated on color and the conditions of light and shade. El Greco and his preceptor Tintoretto were perhaps the first to use a contour as a means of emphasis.

El Greco. "St. John's Vision of the Mysteries of the Apocalypse." (Metropolitan Museum.)

Again in these examples two entirely different approaches to portraiture are shown. In Pollaiuolo's painting the tight outline divides the figure from the background; the hard contours of details within the picture also make them appear as separate entities. In the Velázquez painting the technique of softening and blending is used throughout the picture. The details, brushed in sketchily, do not have the same independent life as those painted by Pollaiuolo.

Pollaiuolo. "Portrait of a Young Woman."
(Poldi Pezzoli Museum, Milan.)

El Greco. "Expulsion from the Temple." (Frick Museum, New York.)

The first illustration shows El Greco's original work, and the two sketches by the author provide a visual analysis of the same picture. The first sketch illustrates a simplification and dehumanization of the theme; this results in a semi-abstract composition suggesting a work by Cézanne. The second shows the dynamic movement of the figures reduced to even more abstract terms.

9. Evolutions in Design

The following analyses of famous paintings end our discussion of classic painting. The intervening styles between Renaissance and Baroque painters and the modern Impressionists are not specifically treated in this book because no basically new painting technique was introduced by the so-called Classic Revival painters (Neo-Classicists) or Romanticist painters.

In bridging the gap between the old and new schools of painting, a study of basic design showing that certain identical elements exist in most styles of painting, regardless of period, proves interesting. These illustrations were chosen not at random but because they possessed inherently "modern" qualities. Many medieval paintings, on account of their frequently primitive or rather grotesque aspects, have a contemporary look to our eyes. Similarly the idioms of many Manneristic or Baroque painters (seen in other illustrations here) have points in common with the art of the present day. The Renaissance style, however, or any other style which is built upon harmonious relationships, and which is static rather than dynamic in nature, is less suited to this kind of "translation."

These analyses of paintings demonstrate how a motif can be reduced to abstract or semi-abstract terms. During this process, certain losses naturally occur, but certain pictorially dynamic gains are made. In analogy we may think of a tree first adorned with all its summer foliage, then stripped to its winter nakedness, when its basic structure is revealed.

El Greco. "View of Toledo." (Metropolitan Museum of Art.)

A similar attempt at simplification has been made here. The original "View of Toledo" is presented, and with it two analytical sketches which show the abstract design and the pattern of light and shade underlying the original painting.

Here the underlying dynamic structure of Grüne-wald's painting is demonstrated in the analytic sketch.

Mathias Grünewald. "Crucifixion." Detail. (Isenheim Altar, Colmar, France.)

Analytic sketch by the author. In this composition objects are viewed simultaneously from different eye levels; thus the perspective is similar to that used by primitive painters. However, the structional elements of the objects are stressed here to the exclusion of all embellishments. In a medieval composition, the artist would have included a wealth of decorative detail.

10. Modern Art and Techniques

The old masters had not one-half the scientific means of investigation that we possess today, and for the most part they relied on tradition in selecting and using their materials. Problems of permanence in painting went hand in hand with principles of good craftsmanship, but the methods used were not uniform. While experimentation was not ruled out, it was mainly tradition that guided the early painters. During the second part of the nineteenth century, with the advent of the Impressionists, traditional methods went out of fashion and artists wishing to follow the new trend found themselves at sea and rudderless in regard to painting techniques. Furthermore, many of the traditions that had been handed down from the masters to their pupils or schools of painting were lost. A century ago and during the first decade of this century, most writing in the field of classic painting techniques was filled with misinformation. Even my own teacher, Max Doerner, the author of the famous textbook *Materials of the Artist,* proved to be wrong on many important points. It has taken ceaseless research on the part of many dedicated men to reconstruct the techniques and formulas of the past. Even so, much remains yet to be discovered and proven.

Impressionism. The date on which "modern art" appeared on the scene seems to depend on a personal point of view. Many artists were experimenting with new forms and techniques before modern art as such was ever heard of by the public. There is no doubt, however, that in regard to the use of color the so-called Impressionists (such artists as Monet, Pissarro, and Sisley) brought about the most radical innovations since the time of the

Renaissance. Generally speaking, all paintings before the advent of Impressionism, when representing outdoor scenes, were conceived in terms of "studio light." This means that the paintings were not done directly from nature and did not display a completely natural range of colors as would be seen in sunlight.

The Impressionists brought about a radical change in the use of the palette as well as in the technique of painting. They used the following colors or their equivalents: ultramarine blue, viridian green, ocher, raw and burnt sienna, cadmium yellow and red, the iron oxide reds, alizarin crimson, and white. Black and umber were strictly taboo! In principle the change rested in making the shadows colorful instead of murky and in diffusing the contours of solid objects. Instead of using subdued tonalities, the Impressionists imbued their canvases with bright, singing colors.

Much of the impressionistic work was done in the open. Some of the painters like van Gogh and Cézanne nearly always worked directly from nature; others would sketch outdoors and finish their paintings in the studio. There are certain advantages to be gained from working outdoors, for an impression derived from immediate observation of natural phenomena rather than a remembered one will usually be more realistic and therefore more authentic. However, the old masters never painted in the open, although they made detailed drawings from nature which they kept for reference.

Because of the rapid changes of the effects of light and shade, work outdoors has to progress rapidly, and every impression must be rendered at once. The technique usually employed by the old masters—the use of more or less elaborate underpaintings—did not allow for this. However, in the case of the alla prima technique, it would have been possible had tradition permitted. In point of fact, the characteristic work of the Impressionists is done in alla prima fashion, but, in contrast to the classic method, glazes are entirely absent. Moreover, whereas the classic alla prima painting was always supported by a framework of delineations, "drawing with paint" never appears in impressionistic work.

Techniques. Characteristically, impressionistic rendering is done on a white canvas ground without preliminary underpaintings. Final effects

Claude Monet. "Boats at Argenteuil." (Museum of Fine Arts, Boston.)

The work of Monet is typical of the Impressionist painters working in France at the end of the last century. They brought about the most radical innovations in the use of color since the Renaissance.

are registered at once and the paint is used opaquely. Glazes are almost never evident. An exception to this is to be found in the work of Renoir. This French artist first received training as a porcelain painter, and his familiarity with the glazing technique, unique among the Impressionists, was undoubtedly what led him to use it.

Since impressionistic forms are diffused or lacking in firm delineations, observance of linear perspective becomes immaterial. However, aerial per-

Renoir. "At the Piano." (Museum of Modern Art, New York.)

The technique of Renoir is more interesting and varied than that of other Impressionists. Having been trained as a porcelain painter in his early years, he acquired a thorough knowledge of the use of glazes—a technique very much neglected by the run-of-the-mill Impressionists. Hence he understood how to imbue his paintings with a luminosity that his contemporaries (who used paint opaquely) never produced. However, Renoir's technique differed from that used by the old masters, for it lacked a planned underpainting.

Renoir. "Monet Painting in His Garden at Argenteuil." Detail.
(Wadsworth Atheneum, Hartford, Connecticut.)

Paul Cézanne. "The Seine, Near Paris." (Rhode Island School of Design.)

Although these two paintings were done alla prima (accomplished in one sitting) they do not interpret the classic alla prima technique at all. The white of the canvas, left untouched in many spots, heightens the impression of sketchiness and quick improvisation. The complete lack of detail and concentration on the severely structural presages the cubist style.

Opposite: Cézanne. "Rocky Landscape at Aix." Detail. (Tate Gallery, London.)

spective—the progressive fade-out of colors as they become more distant—was always considered by these painters, and this makes Impressionism to a degree a "non-modern" conception.

Post-Impressionism. The choice of an outdoor range of colors, as introduced by the Impressionists, does not in itself make a painting "modern" according to contemporary usage of the word, but this, coupled with the repudiation of aerial perspective, which came about with the post-Impressionists, does do so. Cézanne, who is often called the father of modern art, was the first Post-Impressionist painter to repudiate the principles of this perspective.

Techniques. In the work of Cézanne, who was the most important originator of the age, the following characteristics are observable: (1) Stress on the structural rather than pictorial image; hence simplification of forms and elimination of detail. (2) Use of almost the same set of colors regardless of the distance of any object painted. (3) Elimination of infinite distance. (Landscape usually terminates in the middle distance, and the line of the horizon never reveals itself.) (4) Simultaneous visualization and depiction of objects from different levels. (5) An "unfinished" manner of painting. The "unfinished" state of a painting contributes to the impression of freshness and spontaneity. The quicker the hand moves, and the less it tries to smooth out and blend detached brushstrokes, the more spontaneous and fresh the painting appears.

Another great Post-Impressionist, van Gogh, worked entirely alla prima (not in the classic manner, however). He used the colors directly as they came from the tubes, without diluting them, applying a heavy impasto throughout the entire canvas in his characteristic sinewy manner.

Opposite: Vincent Van Gogh. "Cypresses." Van Gogh worked entirely alla prima. See text above. (Knoeller-Mueller Foundation, Wassenaar, Holland.)

"Still Life. 1920." Drawing by the author. A play of semi-abstract forms and lines arranged into a harmonious, decorative design.

Cubism. Cubism, the first and most important innovation in the twentieth century, took its cue solely from Cézanne, who evolved it in his later years. Cubism operates along the following principles: (1) It reduces individual shapes of objects to simple geometric forms. (2) It brings the distant planes of the pictorial space close to the picture's plane; this means that it • narrows this space to shallow recesses, thus eliminating the linear and atmospheric aspects of perspective. (3) It involves, as it were, the object with its surrounding space.

Opposite: Picasso. "L'Arlésienne." Picasso painted this cubist portrait in 1912. (Walter L. Chrysler Collection, Museum of Modern Art.)

"Still Life" by the author, constructed according to cubistic principles. Solid objects, simplified to cubes, cylinders, cones, and spheres, are projected onto the void (negative space), thus tying up the composition with a bilateral framework.

These two drawings by the author, made in 1920, show the human figure in the cubistic style which was fashionable in the first and second decades of this century. Unity of design is achieved by the repetition of geometric shapes. If painted, the figures would be kept predominantly in monotones.

101

Georges Braque. "The Yellow Cloth." (Photo: Carnegie Institute.)

One of the most ingratiating examples of so-called "form analyses." Here, color, form, and texture are ingeniously combined into a decorative design. Braque was one of the first artists to use texture for its own sake rather than to characterize a specific tactile quality of an object.

Stuart Davis. "Hot Stillscape for Six Colors."
(The Downtown Gallery, New York.)

This decorative painting employs a full range of colors in a high key. Stress lies on the strident, flat color and the free-swinging design.

A modified cubism, sometimes referred to as "analytic cubism," employs color freely, as well as a variety of decorative effects. In nature, color plays a large part in defining the characteristics of an object, but in a system that aims at unification and simplification color must be reduced to monotones. In analytic cubism as practiced by such artists as Braque this does not apply. Here the decorative value of the color is fully exploited, and extraneous elements are introduced for embellishing the freely invented forms. With

103

These black and white studies by the author demonstrate two different kinds of illumination. The head at left represents the classic type of lighting, and the head at right is lighted to produce a dramatic shadow effect. Classic lighting refers to the type of chiaroscuro that came into general use during the sixteenth century, a system employing only

one light source for the illumination of the entire composition. Light represented as entering from more than one direction is artificial and was thus not favored by the Renaissance painters.

various modifications the decorative cubism conceived some four decades ago still has currency today.

Technique: In cubistic painting the work is usually improvised, and overpainting is employed chiefly as a corrective measure—to improve a passage that has not come off as desired.

Expressionism. Artists such as El Greco or Grünewald can be looked upon as Expressionists simply because exaggerations, distortions, and a general tendency toward dramatization can be found in their work. The expressionistic painter ignores such classic tenets as well-proportioned anatomy, balanced chiaroscuro, and harmonious color relations. He makes sacrifices for the sake of the excessive and the emotional. In Expressionism the non-realistic approach is predicated on exaggerations in the normal proportions of natural or man-made objects, the use of color dictated by one's feeling rather than by an attempt to achieve realism, and the employment of a non-realistic type of lighting.

Colors as seen in nature are of no concern to the painter who follows the expressionistic style. A sky may be painted vermilion red, foliage may be black, or a stone may be purple; in short, any color capable of conveying the painter's emotions can be used. Colors are thus employed to evoke the feeling of drama rather than a verification of objective facts.

Techniques: In point of technique, expressionistic painting may be said to represent sheer anarchy, since the development of the painting rests entirely on improvisation. This implies that a painting moves along by its own impulse, as it were, unpredictably passing through many evolutions until the intentions of the painter are realized. These intentions, it must be said; are erratic, hence, every phase of development may contradict the preceding one. It is obvious that in a procedure such as this, accidental effects become a

Opposite: Georges Rouault. "Head of a Clown." (Museum of Modern Art.)

Rouault uses heavy impasti applied, as a rule, with a palette knife. However in this example, his principal instrument was a brush. The heavy outlines and contours within the motif (which serve mainly to emphasize the design) are painted entirely in black.

Opposite:

Hyman Bloom. "Jew with Torah."
(Smith College Museum of Art.)

The painter has achieved emphasis
with color and texture, or rather,
with *color-texture,* since he has made
no attempt to differentiate between
the textures of different materials.
The paint shows the same impasto
throughout the entire composition.
It is not so much the form that is
conditioned but the color, which is
used in a purely emotional manner.

David Aronson. "Resurrection."
(Niveau Gallery, New York.)

The influence of El Greco is sug-
gested in this conception. The distortions harmonize perfectly with
the lyricism of the scene. Characteristics of Mannerism—disproportions,
ambiguities, eccentricities, disturbed
balance—are ingeniously combined.

Louis Le Nain. "Landscape with Peasants." (National Gallery of Art, Washington.)

This seemingly realistic work closely resembles certain paintings by Manet, yet has an almost surrealistic quality. The frozen attitudes of the rustics suggest neither that they are alive nor that they are mere dummies.

mainstay. Under certain conditions, much of the art of painting today depends on letting the "accidents" happen and then on exploiting the happy ones for all their worth.

In expressionistic painting, work may proceed from one day to another—provided that the surface has not partially solidified. When using the Copal Painting Medium, no ill effects such as cracking or darkening of the paint film can be expected. However, it is not advisable to paint on a surface of appreciable thickness that, although dry on top, has remained wet underneath. Such heavy paint films should be allowed to solidify throughout. Very heavy and rough impasti should be sandpapered before overpainting, unless, of course, the effects of excessive impasti are desirable. A small electric vibrator sander is useful for this purpose, but naturally the paint must be completely dry and hard before this instrument is used.

To improve the adhesion of successive layers it is well first to sand the surface to be overpainted and then brush turpentine on it. After the turpentine has evaporated, the surface should be oiled with the painting medium before overpainting.

Surrealism. Following our aims to discuss styles in terms of technique and aesthetics, it should be stressed that the term "surrealism" applies, in present-day classification, to a certain category of "realistic" painting as well as to a certain type of abstract art. Of course, there are variations which become difficult to categorize, but all surrealist paintings have one characteristic in common, namely, *the preoccupation with the improbable.* Surrealism is the art of the fantastic, but its fantasy is of a special kind. Fantastic art can have many aspects: it can be romantic, mystic, mythological, allegorical, and so on. But when we classify a style as "surrealist," this category must carry the imprint of irrationality and improbability in regard to its subject matter.

The subject matter in surrealistic art, the storytelling, is the vortex of the style, and images are generally seen in "sharp focus." An object viewed in this manner appears to be more potentially "real," and when the "real" thing is seen out of context, there is a clash between its faculality on one hand, and its absurd locus on the other. For example, an ear on a human head ap-

111

"The Fir Tree." Drawing by the author.

Here our normal associations receive a severe jolt, for we would never encounter a sail tied to a tree. However, this could very well happen in a dream. Surrealism derives most of its inspiration from the world of the unreal and improbable.

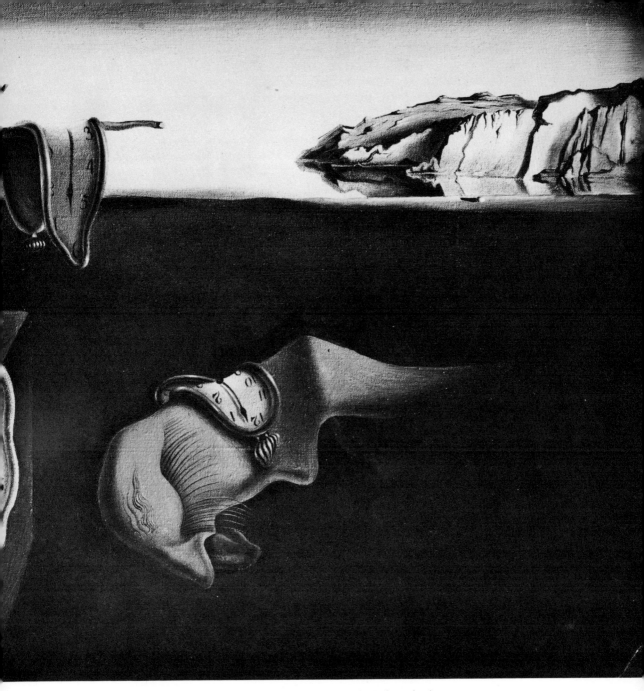

Salvador Dali. "The Persistence of Memory." (Museum of Modern Art.)

The improbable is expressed in this scene in the most telling terms. Everything in it contradicts our experience. The meticulous technique used by Dali, similar to that of the fifteenth-century masters, emphasizes further the air of improbability.

Two paintings belonging to the dehumanized type of surrealism. The eccentric forms bear little or no relation to recognizable objects. In the Tanguy picture an academic pictorial style is combined with a sharp-focus technique. Our inability to associate the objects with anything, animate or inanimate, heightens the feeling of mystery. Although most of the objects are reminiscent of stones and plants, anthropomorphic allusions intrude; hence the mood of ambiguity. In Miró's painting flat patterns are represented in a poster-like style, and a certain humor is revealed in the whimsical forms.

Above: Joan Miró. "The Potato." (Museum of Modern Art.)

Yves Tanguy. "Mama, Papa Is Wounded." (Museum of Modern Art.)

pears quite natural, but when depicted with all its details on a platter (including, perhaps, an earring), it becomes equivocal. And to equivocate with the right emphasis, the object must be largely divested of all "picturesque" qualities. A rock or a tree, or a cloud in the shape of a human head, will have a picturesque rather than a surrealist aspect unless some oblique meanings come into play.

Dealing with the Improbable. Oblique meanings allow a multitude of interpretations, but they may not admit rationalization. Objects realistically conceived and pitched one against another in a contradictory relationship bring about a *dissociation* of ideas. And dissociations do not allow the "probable" to happen. While in fantastic art the improbable is made rational, the opposite holds true in Surrealism. Here, the image of the "real" is weakened to a point where its existence in this dimension becomes absurd. When we consider the fantastic art of Hieronymus Bosch or Brueghel, for example, we must admit that within a mythological "hell" the happenings they depict appear quite believable. On the other hand, a melting watch hanging on a tree limb, as depicted by Dali, has not the slightest chance of being believed.

A study in dissociative ideas, is presented in the drawing of a fir tree with a sail attached. Although the tree might logically serve for the mast of a boat, the sail attached to the living tree renders both the sail and tree out of order. To continue at random, the cast shadow of an object must necessarily correspond with its shape. Should this not be the case, we must assume that order such as we know it on this planet has ceased to exist. The painting by Louis Le Nain, also reproduced in this chapter, represents perfectly real French peasants, yet they seem "unreal" because they appear as "frozen" in motion. Deprived of their inherent characteristics (mobility of human beings), things take on a strange aura of fantasy. Strangely, the most improbable scenes in a Bosch painting usually do not have this aura. Bosch's demons are more real than unreal, inasmuch as they are linked with the human foibles they allegorize.

Technique: In instances where the contents of a painting outweigh the manner in which the work is done, any execution can be used to bring the desired effect, but as a rule an illustrative approach is best. And, since illustra-

tion is preoccupied with details, smoothness of the canvas is essential. On the whole, effects relying on texture and brushstroke and, one could say, even color, are secondary; hence the use of underpainting with all its intricacies is unimportant in a surrealist painting.

Non-objective Art. By definition, non-objective art is not concerned with representation. It resembles "nothing but itself"; hence, all references, however remote, to objects as we know them in nature cease to exist. Two general categories of this type of art are current today—geometric designs and amorphous patterns—demonstrated respectively by the Piet Mondrian and Jackson Pollock paintings in these pages. Much has been written both for and against non-objective art. Essentially such paintings represent. pleasing patterns of color, line, and texture. To read into them deep psychological meanings is perhaps the worst service anyone can do them.

Technique: The technique involved in non-objective painting relies chiefly upon the exploitation of tactile values and a free use of color—free in the sense that the color does not identify an object in a naturalistic manner. Any colors and shapes can be employed, and so can any conceivable technique, including collage.

Collage. Collage is a form of picture making that employs an assembly of heterogeneous materials such as cloth, paper, and whatever other objects may suggest themselves as appropriate to the theme of the picture. In pasting scraps of materials to canvas or board, attractive color and textural designs can be produced. The chief purpose of collage is to enrich the tactile sensations through differentiation of surface appearances. Collage can be non-representative—that is, it may be composed of contrasting materials alone—

Piet Mondrian. "Broadway Boogie Woogie." (Museum of Modern Art.)

The rectangles that make up the entire picture were produced by mechanical means. Any trace of personal sensibility would, according to the doctrine of Purism, appear inappropriate. Since textural effects of surface and color are not intended, this kind of painting can be done on white canvas without preliminary underpaintings.

117

Jackson Pollock. "Ocean Greyness." (The Solomon R. Guggenheim Museum, New York.)

Whereas in the foregoing example methodical, planned procedure is of the essence, paintings belonging to the school of "abstract expressionism" like those of Jackson Pollock are always the product of spontaneous, "automatic" action. The aim of the artist engaged in this type of painting can be limited to color, linear effects, or texture, or it may encompass all these. Overpaints may follow overpaints in endless succession until the desired effects have been achieved. On the other hand, a "desired" effect can also be attained in a single operation.

119

Jean Dubuffet. "Black Countryside."
Collage. (Museum of Modern Art.)

This artist used bits of canvas cut and torn into various
shapes to produce an interesting pattern of outlines,
color, and texture. They were pasted on the canvas
by means of an adhesive.

Opposite: Donald Pierce. "Night Cloud."

The richly variegated textures in this collage were en-
hanced by the introduction of a heavy burlap cut to
an appropriate size and frayed at the edges to make
the cloud formations. This material was painted in
heavy black color and applied against a smooth blue
background.

or some materials may be incorporated into a representational, or semi-representational design for highlighting of tactile effects.

Techniques: The most frequently seen materials in contemporary collages are paper and cloth. The former is usually torn to odd shapes, and various qualities of cloth—fine or coarse-textured—are cut or frayed, their woof and warp pulled and twisted, and then attached onto a board or a canvas with glue. The original color of the materials may be in part, or altogether, altered by overpainting. Many collages are a combination of painted and pasted areas. There are no rules to follow with this technique. Anyone with a good sense of design and an understanding of harmonious colors and textures should easily become proficient.

Details from paintings by the author. Open color again supplants realistic relations of light and shade. The areas in light and shade no longer explain the forms realistically, but are mere suggestions that light and shade exist. The actual form is indicated in outline.

Open Color Painting. In essence, open color painting constitutes a simplification, comparable to shorthand writing. It reduces painting to drawing with color, relieves the heavyhandedness that sometimes weighs down painting with superfluous details and elaborations, and altogether it allows the painter's hand to express itself by means of linear definitions with speed and freedom. This technique cannot be looked upon as a "style" of painting, for it can enter into almost any mode of pictorialization. Tintoretto was among the earliest painters to use it although the method may have been known much earlier. Examples of the open color technique are seen in the details reproduced from a painting by Goya, and in the painting by the

123

Tintoretto. "Doge Alvise." Detail.
(Metropolitan Museum of Art.)

The colors of the background show
within the area of the figure which
Tintoretto outlined in white. This
is, in effect, a pure open color technique.

twentieth-century artist Raoul Dufy. This type of painting has influenced
many present-day fashion artists and magazine illustrators.

Techniques. Since the painter using this technique must rely largely on
delineations, the question arises whether these should be done on top of the
wet paint layer or whether the colors should be allowed to dry before the
motifs are sketched. In the second instance the inexperienced painter will
be able to alter and correct an unsatisfactory design at will without doing
away with the background (which, being dry, will remain intact). However,
such a procedure will result in certain dryness; the designs carried out on

top of it will appear detached from the surface on which they are painted, because they will not incorporate themselves into the dry underlayer of paint. Oiling of the surface in the usual way before starting to paint will not alter this condition. On the other hand, when painting wet-on-wet, a subtle alliance of both the underlying and the superimposed paint will take place. However, in this instance it is difficult to correct an unsatisfactory passage without deleting the complete paint surface. An intermediate procedure would call for doing an underpainting, and, after it dries, painting on it thinly, largely in glazes and scumbles. Sketching onto a thin (glazed) surface is much easier, for in this process the delineations do not engrave themselves as deeply as those executed into a paint layer of appreciable thickness. For most delineations, other than those of a miniature character, a script liner should be used. The paint should either be diluted to a water-color consistency with the painting medium, or made "long" and "soupy," so as to come off the brush in a flowing fashion.

Opposite and right: Goya. "Bullfight." Two details. (Metropolitan Museum of Art.)

Goya frequently used the open color technique. The small figures (measuring in the original painting about five inches) were outlined lightly, and in many areas the color of the background was left uncovered. Following classic precepts, all parts in shade were painted in glazes, but on the light parts white color was used with relative impasto.

Raoul Dufy. "The Great Jockey." (Photo: Perls Galleries.)

Here the color of the background runs through the motifs which are outlined and only slightly modified by additional shades of color. Dufy used the open-color technique systematically and exclusively.

Opposite: Raoul Dufy. "Weighing In at the Deauville Trial." (From *Vanity Fair,* Courtesy Condé Nast.)

Raoul Dufy 1929

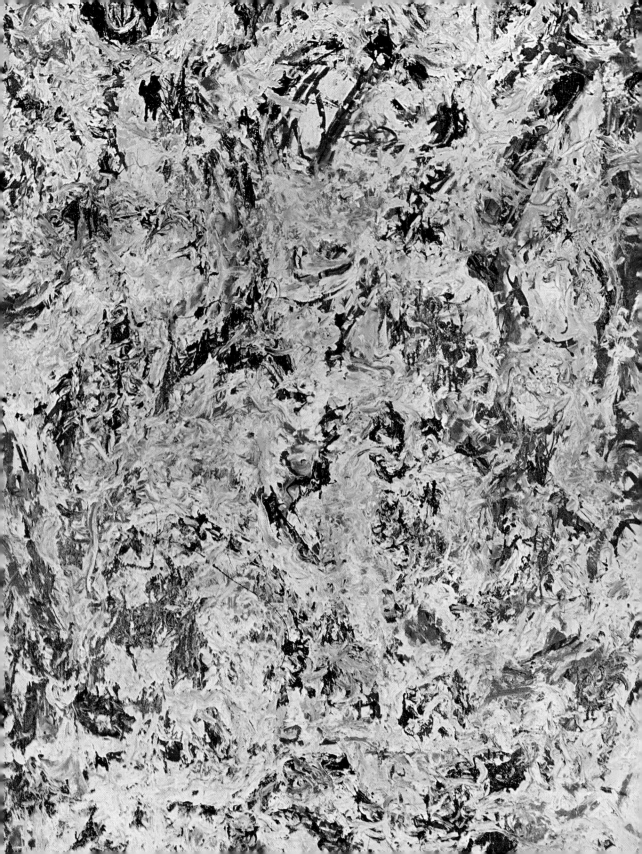

11. Texture

Texture, as a surface quality, can be used for the characterization of objects, or, as it is done today, it can be employed simply for its own sake.

In writing about Bellini, Vasari said: ". . . The texture of skin, of glossy damask, of fur and silk are copied to life." Thus the quality of texture helped to achieve realistic effects. In Dutch paintings of the seventeenth and eighteenth centuries the rendition of an object's texture amounted to a *trompe l'œil*—a "fool the eye" attempt to imitate it. Today this type of painting is commonly referred to as "magic realism." In abstract painting, texture is used merely for its own sake, not to characterize tactile values peculiar to a specific object.

Texture can possess a variety of characteristics. It can be smooth or rough, opaque or transparent. A smooth surface can be either opaque or transparent. In the first instance, a smooth, opaque surface can show brushstrokes (these would have to be extremely shallow, of course), or the surface can be perfectly even. A transparent surface is achieved through glazing. Because of lack of body, textures produced by glazes will of necessity be very delicate.

A rough surface can show great variability in texture, depending on the tools used. A rough texture can also have the quality of transparency if a glaze is applied over it. As to the tools, brushstrokes can be piled up in high impasti in consecutive applications, after each preceding application has completely

Opposite: Jackson Pollock. "Scent." Detail. (Mr. and Mrs. L. Castelli, New York.)
In this type of spontaneous rendition, color and texture play the dominant role. Instead of methodical planning, accident is exploited to the full.

129

Experiment in textures by the author. *(Top)* Sgraffito lines were produced by scraping off light, wet paint with the blade of the palette knife. This uncovered the dark underpainting. *(Bottom)* Rich textures were produced by superimposing one color on top of another color which had been allowed to dry. The final effect was produced by scraping the top color off the underpainting and allowing only traces of it to remain in spots. The scraping was done with sandpaper.

Experiment in textures by the author. The heavy texture was obtained with a thick gesso. This was applied on a dark background and the modeling was done with various tools such as brushes, palette knife, combs, and spatulas.

130

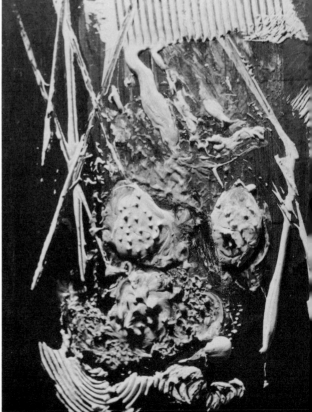

dried. For this purpose certain quick-drying white paints (the so-called "underpainting whites") can be used. Modern acrylic paint, because of its rapid drying, is especially adapted for extreme impasti. Such impasti, however, because they lack the requisite elasticity, should rest on a rigid support (such as Masonite) rather than on a canvas. Other tools useful for execution of impasti are the painting knives.

The roughness of texture can also vary according to the nature of its body. "Short" paint will possess different configurations than "long" paint (see Chapter 3).

The body of paint can also be conditioned or "textured" by adding a variety of foreign materials such as sand, fine gravel, or sawdust. Such granulated surfaces are in evidence in the early work of Braque. They are also often seen in modern, non-objective painting that aims principally at textural effects. For heavy textures, Liquitex Modeling Paste (Permanent Pigments) can be used to great advantage.

Color Effects. Thus far we have considered the surface appearance of an impasto and not its color, except in the instance when glazes and scumbles were mentioned. Other color effects can be produced by spattering. Impasto spatter can be painted by using extra long paint and flipping it off the brush onto the surface of a canvas or panel. Large spatter effects can be obtained by placing the canvas horizontally and squeezing over it a round sable brush well filled with diluted paint. This should be done from some height, so that large drops of paint splash the surface. Paint containing a mixture of a highly polymerized oil behaves like enamel paint; it can be unraveled in thin or thick threads, or splattered in heavy impasto blobs.

The *sgraffito* technique operates on the principle of relieving an underlying color by incising the (wet) color on top of it. Rich "antique" textures can be achieved by painting different colors one on top of another (always allowing the underlying color to dry well first), and then scraping the still wet top color so that only traces of it remain in evidence. Scraping can be done with a tool such as a palette knife, a short hard bristle brush, or any other instrument capable of producing a desirable effect.

Yetta Lustig. "The Seashore." Detail.

The spattering in this painting was made while the surface was still wet. A stiff brush was dipped into a color diluted by varnish and the bristles were flipped with the fingers. In the second area the paint was diluted by a painting medium to a denser consistency, then spattered onto the wet paint surface.

By taking up several colors with a painting knife and mixing them with a few strokes on the canvas, heavy impasti can be painted wet-on-wet in successive applications. The effects of a color impasto produced in this manner are unique and cannot be duplicated by any other means.

Many modern painters use house paints to cover their enormous canvases. This cannot be discussed rationally because the permanence of these colors is dubious. As a matter of fact, in some museums serious problems have already risen as to the restoration and preservation of this kind of work.

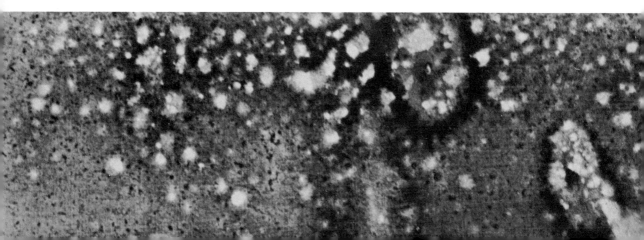

Glossary of Terms

Glossary of Terms

Alla prima: Finishing a painting in one operation while painting wet-on-wet.

Chiaroscuro: Combination of light and shade.

Collage: A composition employing, besides paint, various materials which are attached to the support.

Gesso: A white pigment bound by size or by a suitable adhesive.

Glaze: A transparent film of darker color painted on top of a lighter color.

Gouache: Opaque water color.

Grisaille: Underpainting in grays.

Hygroscopic: Able to absorb moisture.

Impasto: A thick paint application.

Imprimatura: A varnish-diluted color on which alla prima painting is done.

Linear approach: Painting relying largely on delineation.

Linoxyn: The dry skin of linseed oil.

Paint: Pigment suspended in a vehicle.

Paint, long: A material that will tend to seek the level when heaped up.

Paint, short: A material that forms sharp configurations when heaped up.

Painterly approach: Avoidance of delineations and hard definitions in a painting.

Perspective, atmospheric: A fading out of color with the increase of distance in a painting.

Perspective, scientific (also called *empirical* or *linear perspective*): Perspective that relies on the principle that all parallels converge at the vanishing point on the horizon at eye level.

Pigment: Dry color matter.

Polymerization: Grouping (in a liquid) of small molecules to form large molecules.

Resin: Exudates of coniferous trees.

Resin, hard: Exudates of trees now extinct.

Resin, soft: Exudates of living trees.

Siccative: A drying agent.

Size: A solution of glue in water.

Stabilizer: A material added to tube paint to effect a permanent suspension of pigment in oil.

Tooth: Rough quality of a surface.

Varnish: A solution of resin in a volatile liquid.